OMNIBUS PRESS PRESENTS THE STORY OF

'N SYNC

Copyright © 1999 Omnibus Press
(A Division of Book Sales Limited)

Written by: Ashley Adams
Cover and Book Design by: Jade Romigin

US ISBN: 0.8256.1760.X
UK ISBN: 0.7119.7697.X

All rights reserved. No part of
this book may be reproduced in
any form or by any electronic or
mechanical means, including
information storage or retrieval
systems, without permission in
writing from the publisher,
except by a reviewer who
may quote brief passages.

Exclusive distributors:
Book Sales Limited
8/9 Frith Street, London
W1V 5TZ, UK

Music Sales Corporation
257 Park Avenue South
New York City, NY 10010, USA

Music Sales PTY, Ltd
120 Rothschild Avenue
Roseberry, NSW 2018
Australia

To the Music Trade only:
Music Sales Limited,
8/9 Frith Street,
London W1V 5TZ, UK

Photo Credits:
Bernhard Kuhmstedt/ Retna Ltd/ Retna Pictures:
Title Page, 6,9,10,13,14,17,18,19,21,
22,26,27,28,29,34,36,38,41,42,43,47
Tim Hale/ Retna Ltd, USA: 3,4,5
Jen Lowery: 7,25 bottom, 33, 37,45,48
Steve Granitz/ Retna Ltd: 25 top
Melanie Edwards/ Retna Ltd, USA: 39
Kelly Swift: 25 middle, 30 top, 30 middle

Front Cover Photograph: Bernhard Kuhmstedt/ Retna Pictures
Back Cover Photograph: Bernhard Kuhmstedt/ Retna Pictures
Printed in the United States of America by
Vicks Lithograph and Printing Corp.

'N Sync is one of the hottest groups of the late Nineties—and with their endless energy and talent, they promise to be one of the top musical acts of the new millennium. Justin Timberlake; J.C. Chasez; Chris Fitzpatrick; Joey Fatone, Jr.; and Lance Bass have taken the international pop scene by storm with their irresistible blend of five-part harmonies, beautiful melodies, catchy dance beats, and unforgettable live shows.

They may be young, but 'N Sync are no newcomers to the entertainment world. All five members of this group have quite a list of credits to their names—including movies, stage and television shows, *The Mickey Mouse Club*, and much more. And all this before the fateful day in 1995 when they all came together in Orlando, Florida to form 'N Sync! Practice, dedication, and a very "in sync" vibe soon paid off, and the group was off to Europe to record their debut album and take off on the roller coaster ride of a lifetime.

Today 'N Sync have two multiplatinum U.S. albums, *'N Sync* and *Home for Christmas*, and a third on the way. Their singles "I Want You Back," "Tearin' Up My Heart," and "(God Must Have Spent) A Little More Time on You" have topped the charts worldwide. Their high-energy concerts sell out night after night. But they still take time before every single show to meet a new group of fans. The secret to 'N Sync's success is that they don't do it for the fame and fortune—they do it all for their fans.

GIDDY UP

'N Sync is a dream of a group, and so it makes sense that they came together in a land of fantasy. Chris Fitzpatrick, an energetic young performer at Universal Studios in Orlando, Florida, had an idea that grew and grew while he was busy singing and dancing his days away. He wanted to put together a musical group that could blend five-part harmonies with upbeat pop and present it all with the entertainment sensibility he'd learned onstage at the theme park. Chris would describe the Orlando scene years later to MTV's John Norris in a December 4, 1998, interview, saying, "It really is a melting pot of talent because there's so much music, theater, so much opportunities. It really is a small town because everybody knows each other because of the business."

Chris broached the subject of his concept to fourteen-year-old Justin Timberlake, whom he had met during auditions. Chris had heard Justin sing, and had recognized the kind of talent that would help his dream become a reality. Justin, although barely a teenager, was no newcomer to the entertainment world and had earned his stripes on television as one of the cast of Disney's new version of *The Mickey Mouse Club*. Justin liked the idea of forming a band, and quickly enlisted fellow former mouseketeer J.C. Chasez, whose soulful voice was a perfect complement to Justin's funky style and Chris's soprano. Years later, J.C. was full of good things to say about the *MMC* during 'N Sync's America Online chat. "I would say that it was the experience of a lifetime," he raved. "We got to do all spectrums of the business, not just singing and dancing, but acting too. It's something that will be with us for the rest of our lives, it was a great experience."

It wasn't long before Joey Fatone, a Brooklyn native, fell into the fold. Joey, a charismatic performer with a love of doo-wop, had shared the stage with Chris in Universal's *Beetlejuice Graveyard Revue*, and knew J.C. through some of his own high school pals who had also been on the *MMC*. The guys were ready to rumble, but they were missing a key ingredient: a bass voice to round out the mix and complete the harmony.

{four}

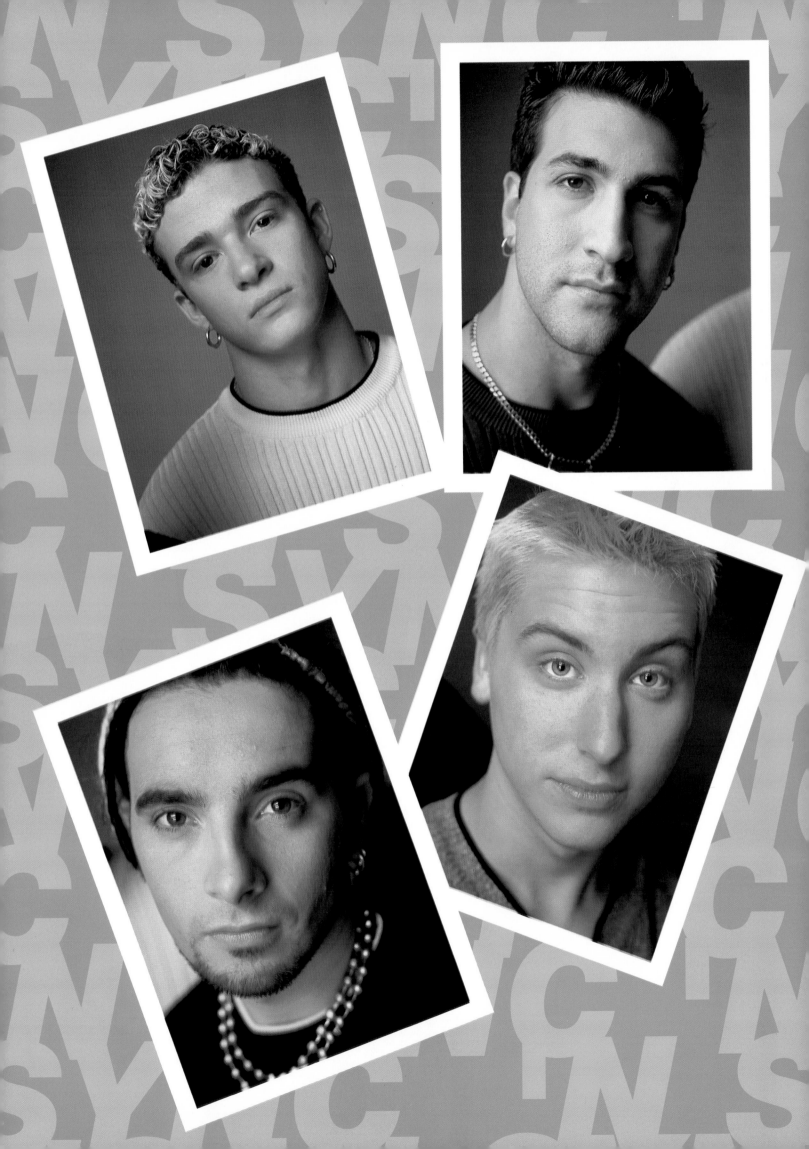

Justin picked up the phone and contacted his former vocal coach back home in Memphis, Tennessee, to see if he might be able to suggest anyone. And that is how Lance Bass, a day-care worker in Clinton, Mississippi, found himself on a plane to Florida to meet up with the foursome who wanted to be a fivesome. As soon as they all met, the guys knew they had the perfect mix of voices . . . and personalities!

They set to work practicing and putting together an act. They spent hours each day working on what would soon become one of the hottest bands to hit the charts. They rehearsed whenever and wherever they could, often juggling time in between their day jobs and singing into the wee hours of the morning. It didn't take them long to realize they were on to something good. But they needed one more thing: a name. Justin's mother complimented the fledgling group on how in sync they were vocally, and later as she was fooling around with the letters of the boys names, trying to come up with a name for the band, she discovered that the guys really were 'N Sync. The last letters of the members first names (using Lance's nickname Lansten) formed a band name everyone agreed was ace. It was time to giddy up!

The unknown 'N Sync crew knew they needed to get the attention of someone in the entertainment industry with some clout, and so they decided to do something a little different. Instead of sending out demo tapes like every other wannabe group, they recorded a video demo package, wisely realizing that their energy, dancing skills, and above all their ability to entertain were an important part of their appeal. They printed their own posters, chose their own wardrobe, worked out their own choreography, and sent the demo—which included a cover version of the Beatles' hit "We Can Work It Out"—out into the world.

And work it out they did. When the band first formed, Justin would years later recall to *Entertainment Weekly* in its March 5, 1999, cover story on 'N Sync, "We'd perform for whoever would listen. We'd be in the middle of a restaurant saying, 'Can we sing for you?'" A year after 'N Sync was born—a year full of performing anywhere, anyhow, and honing their skills—their demo package grabbed the attention of an entrepreneur named Louis Pearlman.

Lou Pearlman made his first couple of million through launching an aviation company that flew top business executives from the airport into New York City in helicopters, so that they wouldn't have to waste time sitting in traffic in a stretch limo. He came into contact with the grandfather of the boy bands, New Kids on the Block, when the group chartered one of his jets. The businessman couldn't believe that these "Kids" were successful enough to afford his services, and picked up the phone to call his cousin, Art Garfunkel of Simon & Garfunkel fame, to get an insider's scoop on the young upstarts. Pearlman had always had a love of music, and years later, with the memory of the New Kids in his mind, he decided to take none other than the Backstreet Boys under his wing with former New Kids tour manager Johnny Wright.

'N Sync joined up with Pearlman and Wright, and signed a recording deal with BMG Germany. Wait a minute, you might say—why Germany? Well, back in 1996 pop wasn't the sound of the moment in the United States. Grunge, punk, and alternative ruled the airwaves, and five clean-cut pop stars who could sing *a cappella* and dance like pros just weren't the ticket. Johnny Wright realized that in order to record the kind of album 'N Sync should record, they had to do it in Europe. He also knew that the band could develop their act and hopefully become very popular in the more pop-orientated musical climate abroad.

Lance later explained to *Entertainment Weekly Online* why the band went all the way across the Atlantic Ocean to start their career, saying, "In Europe there's just an abundance of groups and soloists. They have maybe four times as many of everything. They have four Mariah Careys, four Backstreet Boys. And they love everybody.

That's why everyone kind of goes to try out new stuff. Even now, Michael Jackson and Madonna release their material first in Europe before they bring it here, just to kind of see what it's going to do."

So it was that the 'N Sync five landed in recording studios in Hamburg, Munich, and in Stockholm, Sweden's Cheiron Studios. Joey would later tell *Billboard* in its March 20, 1999, issue, "We liked the sound that producers like Denniz Pop and Max Martin were doing," adding, "They have an original sound . . . a very full, upbeat Swedish pop sound that we like." Pop, Martin, and Kristian Lundin–the Swedish producers and writers behind "I Want You Back" and "Tearin' Up My Heart"–have also put hits together for the likes of the Backstreet Boys, U.K. sensation Five, and fellow Scandinavians Robyn and Ace of Base.

But what made 'N Sync stand out in such a busy European music scene? Why did they make it so big, so fast, in Germany, Austria, Switzerland, and Sweden? Johnny Wright told *Billboard* in its March 20, 1999, issue, "Many of the big teen acts at the time in Germany were not singing live. They were all lip-syncing. And 'N Sync wasn't. They can sing. So they would always sing songs *a cappella*, as well as with music. It was important that they not come across as another one of those manufactured poster boy acts." Jan Bolz, the managing director of BMG Ariola Munich, emphasized in *Billboard* that 'N Sync had something special, saying, "We could not have done this with a German band. Americans are great entertainers."

By the way, the idea to use the * in the '*N Sync* logo came from a very unusual source. The band met up with psychic Uri Geller while they were in the U.K., and he reportedly advised the guys to put a star on their record to ensure its success–looks like it worked! That's one psychic I'd carry on consulting.

'*N Sync*, the album, was first released in Europe in May 1997. The first single "I Want You Back" was already riding high on the German charts. Ready or not, the time had come for 'N Sync to take off on the roller coaster ride of their lives. Little did they know it was destined to last a long, long time with barely a chance to catch their breaths. The hot new group toured for the next two years in Europe, Asia, South Africa, and Mexico with Justin's mother Lynn and Lance's mother Diane (an English teacher) as tour chaperones. "We took care of them, fussed at them if they weren't getting enough rest or food," Diane reminisced to *People Online* in its February 8, 1999, issue. "It was exhausting." Exhausting, but energizing at the same time. 'N Sync knew they had what it took to conquer their homeland, and the time was right–America was tired of alternative, and ready for gold old-fashioned talent and a bit of fun. Groups like the Backstreet Boys and the Spice Girls had knocked on the door, and the welcome mat was out for the return of pop.

The U.S. *'N Sync* album was released in America in March 1998 on RCA, and featured a different track listing than its European counterpart, including some extra tracks that were recorded in studios in New York and at Trans Continental Studios in Orlando. Trans Continental, today the headquarters of Lou Pearlman and Johnny Wright, is located just down the road from Sea World. Nowadays, there is definitely a unique vibe at Trans Con. The Los Angeles *Times* January 24, 1999, article by Geoff Boucher entitled "The Making of Heartthrobs Inc." noted that the Orlando office "is inevitably described by everyone involved as a family-style workplace far removed from the cutthroat music industry hubs of Los Angeles and New York," and quoted executive Jay Marose as saying, "It took me a few weeks to get used to everyone hugging each other in the halls." Trans Continental has a few more pop acts up its sleeve, ready to hit the road and the charts, namely C Note, Take 5, Lyte Funkie Ones, and girl band Innosense.

But back to 'N Sync's American debut. The band enjoyed their fair share of success at first, but it wasn't the same as the stardom and fame they had become accustomed to in Europe. In fact, it was a relief of sorts to be able to walk down the street without being recognized, and the guys reveled in a bit of normality in between gigs, radio promotions, and magazine interviews with major music industry magazines as well as top teen publications. "I Want You Back" hit the singles chart, and the video began to be played more and more frequently on MTV. 'N Sync joined the likes of Mariah Carey, Paula Cole, Olivia Newton-John, and Matchbox 20 for a benefit concert at Radio City Music Hall on May 31; the concert's proceeds went to PAX, a non-profit organization that tries to put a stop to gun violence in America. This wasn't the band's first—nor would it be the last—piece of charity work. 'N Sync performed at Charity '98 in Oberhausen, Germany, to raise funds for sick children. They were featured on a charity single called "Children Need a Helping Hand" which was a Number One hit on the German charts.

'N Sync took to the road on a full-on North American tour which began on the Fourth of July in St. Petersburg, Florida, and went on to touch down in many Canadian cities, as well as dates at Chicago's House of Blues, the Warner Theatre in Washington D.C., and the Kansas State Fair. The sound of 'N Sync was beginning to take a grip on the U.S. As Johnny Wright told *Billboard* in its March 20, 1999, issue, "The European producers were creating something fresh and new. And Americans supported it. It was a clean-cut sound. And the act supported that. Parents liked it, too. So the sound took off here, too. In Europe, it wasn't a new sound, it was just pop music." Although the 'N Sync five didn't take the States by storm the moment they stepped off the plane, it wouldn't be long before they were to become a major sensation.

It was the July 18, 1998, "'N Sync In Concert" Disney special, however, that really broke the ice. The concert was originally supposed to be a Backstreet Boys special, but just two weeks before the scheduled taping, Backstreet backed out of the gig, and 'N Sync were only too happy to take the slot. "Even after we filmed it, we just thought it was a little concert," Chris told *Entertainment Weekly* in its March 5, 1999, cover story. "I was like, 'Well, that was cool. Now we gotta

go work on our *careers*." Barely a month after the concert, *'N Sync* the album rocketed its way right into the Top Ten. And there it would stay for a long, long time. At the beginning of August 1998 'N Sync's album broke into the *Billboard* charts at Number Nine, one place below the Backstreet Boys who were at Number Eight, and one slot above none other than Will Smith.

'N Sync the album was a gold mine of the many musical strengths of the group. The opening track, "Tearin Up My Heart," was destined to be a major hit. Aside from the song's catchy melody and

irresistible beat, the lyrics (*It's tearin' up my heart, When I'm with you /And when we are apart, I feel it too / And no matter what I do I feel the pain / With or without you*) are a perfect testament to the anguish of young love. As J.C. said in the *'N the Mix* official home video, "Believe it or not, there's a great message in the song that I think everybody can relate to." Joey describes it in simple terms, as a "knot—butterflies in your stomach." And we've all been there. The album also offers some sweet love songs. "(God Must Have Spent) A Little More Time on You" is a standout track, and you'll find that all of the band members cite it as one of their favorites. Its heartfelt lyrics (*In all of creation, all things great and small / You are the one who surpasses them all*) are a joy to sing. As Justin says on the *'N Sync* Enhanced CD, the song "relates to me a lot just because I'm a very spiritual person." He explains, "I think it's a wittier way of saying to someone how special they are." "For the Girl Who Has Everything" is another sweet ballad. As Joey says in the *'N the Mix* official home video, "Being in love—it's a gift, and a special gift. You can't put a price on it."

The thirteen songs showcase the five-strong singing force of 'N Sync's many vocal styles and ranges. Their harmonizing is, of course, a constant strength. "You Got It" is a beat-driven dance track with a smattering of street-corner doo-wop thrown in. A Stevie Wonder influence can be heard on "I Just Wanna Be with You" and "Everything I Own" brings Michael Jackson to mind at times.

Lance told *Entertainment Weekly Online* in its October 20, 1998, article entitled "Tearin' Up the Charts" about the cover song "Sailing," which was originally a hit by Christopher Cross. "It's just one of those songs that you've always loved, but if you tried to name the artist you probably couldn't. We didn't know who sang it when we first decided to do it." The band felt the song would be "vocally challenging" with its many parts, and as Lance went on to say, "So we did it almost two years ago and it's been our baby since. It's been like our pride and joy."

The album closes with the only song the band helped to write, "Giddy Up." It's the funkiest track by far, featuring the sound of an old scratched record. Chris described "Giddy Up" during his January 5, 1999, Yahoo chat, saying, "It's about having fun. Getting off your butt and have fun. That's pretty much the theme of the song." It's a fitting conclusion to an album that would prove that 'N Sync planned to have a lot of fun in their own country.

'N Sync rounded off the summer with a few choice appearances, to say the least. The band had a fantastic time on August 28 helping multimillionaire and entrepreneur Richard Branson promote the opening of his new Virgin Megastore in New York City's Union Square. The band joined British songstress Petula Clark (who had the boys sing along with her hit "Downtown") on top of a red London double-decker bus. The party drove through the streets of the city, delighting expectant fans and surprised New Yorkers alike, and Richard Branson's trademark grin seemed even wider than usual when 'N Sync got the crowds going. And they certainly know how to do that. Cheerleader-style chants rev up the audience to the tune of "When I say "'N" y'all say "Sync"–"N!" . . . "SYNC!" . . . "'N!" . . . "SYNC!" It's hard for the boys to resist playing with the crowd, and Justin has been known to shout out the command, "Now scream!" to tremendous effect. 'N Sync also performed at the Miss Teen USA pageant, and appeared on the *Tonight Show with Jay Leno* on September 10 along with *Ally McBeal* star Calista Flockhart. They finished off the month with a spot on MTV's *Total Request Live*, much to the delight of the horde of screaming fans outside the Times Square, New York City, studio.

On October 14, 'N Sync were pinching themselves as they set out on tour with one of their favorite artists, Janet Jackson. In an October 6 *MTV News* interview, Chris raved about the opportunity to be a part of Janet's Velvet Rope tour, saying, "We don't care if we get booed off the stage. We're just gonna be like, 'What's up Janet. You're welcome. They're ready for you.'" Needless to say, the band did not get booed off the stage. On Yahoo, Lance described Janet Jackson as "one of the nicest persons in the world . . . very down to earth and humble." Joey has admitted to having a crush on her! One of the highlights of the tour was the 'N Sync and Janet *a cappella* duet of Stevie Wonder's "Overjoyed." In addition to the band's admiration for Janet's talent and professionalism, the stint on her tour gave them a chance to warm up for their very own headlining tour.

But first: a few more TV appearances, including a November 4 German chart show and a November 6 *Tonight Show with Jay Leno*, this time with Courtney Thorne-Smith. The band's favorite television experience? Has to be the Rosie O'Donnell show. Lance raved about 'N Sync's appearance on the daytime talk show during his February 22, 1999, Yahoo chat, saying, "It was great. It was a dream come true. As everyone knows, she is like my favorite person in the world. I was really looking forward to doing it and it was everything I hoped for and more. And she surprised me by bringing in Lucy Arnez, because as she knows, my favorite actress is Lucille Ball."

'N Sync kicked off the tour, literally, at the Honolulu, Hawaii, Oia football championship pregame concert at the Aloha Stadium. 'N Sync sang the national anthem to more than 15,000 people that night. Fittingly, the official start of their tour was on November 17 in the band's hometown, Orlando, Florida, with a hot new artist as their opening act: a young lady named Britney Spears whose album . . . *Baby One More Time* was soon to make a huge dent in the charts. Britney was no stranger to at least part of the band: she had been the youngest Mouseketeer on *The Mickey Mouse Show* when Justin and J.C. were wearing their ears. So, it was a reunion of sorts. Rumors started flying that Justin and Britney were dating, but both pop stars laughed it off, claiming to be more like brother and sister than boyfriend and girlfriend.

'N Sync teamed up with the Backstreet Boys to record a benefit single released in November called "Let the Music Heal Your Soul," the work of a team of vocal artists who adopted the name Bravo All Stars. A charity organization called the Nordoff-Robbins Music Therapy Foundation was to receive the proceeds in order to help autistic and disabled kids.

Inevitably, there is a lot of hype about competition between the Backstreet Boys and 'N Sync, but the guys in 'N Sync say that's just what it is: hype. "There's no animosity," Johnny Wright insisted in the November 1998 issue of *Teen People*. "The more vocal groups there are, the better it is, because the more variety (the fans) have, the more great music they could

have." Of course, the fact that 'N Sync shared the common thread of Louis Pearlman and Johnny Wright helped fuel the comparisons between the two groups. Justin told *Teen People*, "When we put our group together—and we were together for about six months before we met Johnny—I didn't even know who the Backstreet Boys were." When the Backstreet Boys let Johnny Wright go as their manager, rumors abounded that it was because of 'N Sync's success that BSB didn't want to work with Johnny anymore. "It could have been over us; it could have been over money. I'd rather not know," J.C. told the Los Angeles *Times*. "It's none of my business." Journalists especially liked to hold the two bands up against one another. The Los Angeles *Times*, in its January 7, 1999, issue, gave a rather jaded review of the band's Universal Amphitheatre concert comparing the fivesome to BSB: "Judging from the intensity of the teen screams throughout 'N Sync's official L.A. concert debut, 'N Sync has successfully challenged the swoony sovereignty of the Backstreet Boys," columnist Natalie Nichols wrote, adding, "And they've done it largely by following the same formula."

Regardless, both groups are on top of the world, and Johnny Wright is just the right fit for 'N Sync. As a manager, he gives his all, and expects the same of his acts. As he told *Entertainment Weekly*, "I'm lucky to have acts that are hungry. I tell them straight up: When that window's open, you have to put whatever you got through it -and let's not be worried about vacations and all this other stuff." He described his very hands-on approach, saying, "I'm the artist-develop-ment person; I'm the guy who swept the teddy bears off the stage. . . . When I walk out with 'N Sync, the fans know who Johnny Wright is."

On November 10 the band's very own Christmas album entitled *Home for Christmas* was released. As any 'N Sync fan knows, the guys in the band are crazy about Christmas; and, as if the album wasn't enough of a gift to their fans, they also put out their own book, *'N Sync: The Official Book*, and their own official home video called *'N the Mix* on the very same day. *Home for Christmas* features both traditional Christmas songs, including "O Holy Night" which the band sings a cappella, "The Christmas Song (Chestnuts Roasting on an Open Fire," and "The First Noel," as well as many original tracks. It was recorded mainly at Trans Continental Studios, as well as Pennsylvania's Get Wild Studios, New York's The Loft, Los Angeles's Larrabee North Studios, Nashville's The Hot Closet, and even as far afield as FM Studio in Frankfurt, Germany. Justin and J.C. share writing credits on the single "Merry Christmas, Happy Holidays," a song whose video debuted on MTV on November 29. Christmas spirit fills the video, which features the guys riding a sleigh (with Joey at the helm) and feeding the homeless. It also includes a cameo appearance by Gary Coleman, who plays an elf! "Not just anybody can put out a Christmas record," J.C. told *Teen People* in its November 1998 cover story on the band. "(You) have to have somewhat of a following for people to want to pick it up. And that made us feel very good."

But before Christmas comes Thanksgiving, and 'N Sync celebrated the holiday in style, joining Macy's famous Thanksgiving Day parade, along with fellow musical celebrities Chicago and Monica. Lance couldn't get over being a part of the tradition he had watched every year on his grandmother's TV. The band, accompanied on their float by a giant yellow M&M, braved the weather with fur-lined hoods and clear umbrellas.

December was a busy, busy month for the 'N Sync five. How they ever had time to do their Christmas shopping we will never know. The band joined Shania Twain, Edwin McCain, the Goo Goo Dolls, Boyz II Men, Monica, Lauryn Hill, Eagle-Eye Cherry, the Bryan Setzer Orchestra, Barenaked Ladies, Shawn Mullins, and 98° at the annual Jingle Ball concert at Radio City Music Hall. The concert is sponsored by New York City radio station Z-100, and it is all in the name of fun and a very good cause. The proceeds from the show go to charity groups Share, the Refugee Project, and the Lupus Foundation of America. All of the participating groups put on a good show, and Barenaked Ladies earned a few extra squeals from the audience when they made a joke about having caught a peak at 'N Sync in the buff in the changing room. They also appeared on *Regis & Kathie Lee*, *The Disney Christmas Show*, and in *Walt Disney World's Very Merry Christmas Parade*.

All of this while their tour went on! The band did take a two-week

break to spend some time with family and friends during the holiday season, but got right back on stage two days after Christmas.

So what did the guys get for Christmas? More than a few awards, that's for sure. The band (all except J.C.) got 'N Sync-inspired tattoos late one night after being presented with their first Platinum album live on Canadian television. "I Want You Back" won Best Dance Clip and Best Dance New Artist Clip at the Billboard Music Video Awards. 'N Sync presented the Bee Gees with a Lifetime Achievement Award at the 1998 Billboard Music Awards held December 7, 1998, at the MGM Grand in Las Vegas. They also served as presenters and winners alike at the American Music Awards where they handed an award over to Garth Brooks and picked one up for Best New Artist. The band didn't do too badly at the America Online Entertainment Asylum's "You've Got Fans" online awards, in which they won CD of the Year and Favorite Musical Artist; Justin won two awards all on his own: Hottest Male and Sexiest Newcomer! In just one week in December, both their debut and Christmas albums were in the Top Ten at the same time, and the two albums combined sold 400,000 copies in only seven days. All in all, the understatement of the decade is that it was a pretty good year for the boys.

'N Sync started the New Year off with a bang, playing to a sold-out crowd in the party city of the world, Las Vegas. They now had hot new girl band B*Witched, straight from Ireland, as their support act, and the show was better than ever. As Justin said during a Yahoo chat, "You can imagine them on St. Patrick's Day. They're sweet girls. . . . Every opening act we've had has been a joy to work with."

The band showed their seemingly endless supply of energy and their love for touring when they set out on yet another full-on tour with new support act Tatyana Ali. Starting off once again in Florida, the boys hit the road with performances scheduled for almost every night in March, April, and May, playing cities in dozens of states. This time they brought a new pal on the road with them—Chris's dog, a pug named Busta.

The New York *Times* March 17, 1999, review of the Nassau Coliseum concert by columnist Ann Powers was complimentary of the band's showmanship. It said, "'N Sync evoked a different sort of entertainment: the Broadway-style revue. Like rock-and-roll, this show linked back to the circus and the vaudeville hall, but it was much more stylized and blatantly spectacular than rock."

So what exactly is it about the 'N Sync live experience that makes their concerts so special? And how do they remain in sync onstage every night, and on the road every day? The guys pride themselves on working very hard to fulfill their goal of keeping the audience entertained from the moment the show begins. The nonstop energy of 'N Sync's live show is an experience the band's fans won't soon forget.

'N Sync's fantastic dance routines are the result of teamwork—they do use professional choreographers, but the five performers contribute their own steps and ideas to the mix. As anyone who has been lucky enough to see 'N Sync live in concert can tell you, the collaboration definitely works. They make it look easy on stage because they've put so much time and effort into preparing themselves. "I was the worst dancer when I joined the group!" Lance confessed during his online Yahoo chat session on December 2, 1998. "I spent hours with a choreographer every day so I could learn." The guys still spend eight to ten hours a day before they go on tour perfecting their moves, and brush up before each concert at the sound check. In fact, although all of the guys have buff bods and are obviously in great physical shape, none of them work out—they get more than enough exercise performing!

The guys add their very own special touches to their ever-changing choreography, including ultra-entertaining gymnastic moves and special gestures that go along with the lyrics. Needless to say, the fans take it all in, and are soon following along. 'N Sync's live performances are definitely interactive. The fans, aside from singing along to every word in every song, hold up signs for the band to see when the house lights go on. The band likes to have a little fun with the audience, too, and has been known to squirt the crowd with water guns. The latest tour opened up with the five 'N Syncers in shiny space jumpsuits, their faces covered in white helmets as the strains of Darth Vader's *Star Wars* theme song filled the air. The band also incorporates cover versions of other artists' songs into its live show, including Kool and the Gang's hit "Celebration," "That Thing You Do" from the Tom Hanks movie, and even a Jackson Five medley.

'N Sync are pros at keeping their audience enthralled, and there is so much packed into their stage show it's no wonder fans travel from city to city to see them perform over and over again. The group wisely wants to keep their fans' attention every second, and surprises are the name of the game. As Lance says in the *'N the Mix* official home video, "When you look at us onstage, every song has a different feel to it." J.C. says he wants the fans to gasp, "Did you see that?" Fun and originality are important to this band. J.C. told *Faces in Pop* magazine, "We're all into what we do so much. We all love to sing, dance, write—do whatever we can to entertain. That's

what we share. This has never been about the fame or the money to us. It's always been about entertaining."

Aside from all of the rehearsing and planning that goes into their show, how do the boys prepare themselves for the adrenaline rush of running out onto the stage to the roar of the crowd each night? The band members de-stress and loosen up right before a show with a little help from their wardrobe assistants who double as licensed masseuses. That prepares them physically, but what about mentally? "We always pray before a show," Justin told *SuperTeen* magazine in its June 1999 issue. "We pray in the dressing room.

We get all the crew together and pray. . . . I say a prayer that we do a good show and we're safe. Then we get into a huddle and pump each other up before we go out on stage."

Any 'N Sync fan knows that the band is, without a doubt, five individual parts of a very highly tuned machine when it comes to their music. Believe it or not, they get along with the same syncopation behind the scenes. It's one-for-all and all-for-one. J.C. discussed the band's outlook during 'N Sync's April 24, 1998, American Online chat, stating, "Usually we agree but . . . if we don't, we talk it out and deal with it. Once we come to a decision on something, we all back it up completely."

The guys claim to get along like brothers, and that includes playing practical jokes on each other. A few standout pranks have been squeezing toothpaste into an unsuspecting band member's ear, or filling an empty tennis shoe with shaving cream. There has been at least one whipped-cream war, and a very tired Lance fell asleep in his dressing room once only to wake up covered in his Beanie Baby collection. On an airplane J.C. decided to take advantage of the down time and indulge in his favorite hobby—you guessed it, a little shut-eye—only to wake and discover Polaroids of himself sound asleep and covered in candy. Even the tubes of Rollos his prankster friends stuck in his ears didn't wake him up! "We're a family–just like any other perfectly dysfunctional family," J.C. laughingly told *Hit Sensation* magazine.

The band's tour bus is their home away from home. The guys chill out by watching movies on the road. Some of their favorites are *Austin Powers* and *Spinal Tap*. Joey's all-time favorite flick is *Willie Wonka and the Chocolate Factory*. What about rock 'n roll style misbehavior? Has 'N Sync ever been thrown out of a hotel for trashing the rooms or throwing television sets out the window like some rock stars? Of course not. As Joey disclosed during a Yahoo chat, "We've never been kicked out of one . . . but one time in London they told us that we couldn't come back because there were too many fans outside the hotel."

Even though the five 'N Syncers are extremely close, they still miss their friends and family back home. Justin told his fans on Yahoo that he is "very, very, very close" to his family, adding, "I miss them a lot on the road. I talk to my mother every day. I think I became closer to my family when I couldn't see them a lot. I never knew how much I valued family time until I didn't have it. I'm a family man." All of the guys are in close contact with home, sweet home, however–they would be lost without their cell-phones! Justin told *SuperTeen* magazine that the guys like to record silly messages on their phones, like, "Hi, I'm on stage right now, so as soon as I get done singing 'Tearin' Up My Heart' I'll call you back." The 'N Sync crew are all plugged in to the Internet as well. "I've got a computer that I use to go online at least once a week and say hello to all my friends. We always get in a chat room and I get to talk to like fifty of my friends at the same time, which is a lot easier on the cell bill," Lance told *Entertainment Weekly Online*. "And I go into 'N Sync chat rooms, and of course they never believe it's me." So, fans, keep on your toes!

Speaking of fans . . . 'N Sync have a very close relationship with their fans, and no matter how successful they are, they plan to keep it that way. Before every show they do a "Meet and Greet" with forty or fifty fans, just to get to know their audience. They consider it just as much a privilege to meet the people they will be performing for as the fans find it a thrill to meet their favorite artists in person.

Fans—especially girls!—will go to all lengths to meet 'N Sync. Sneaking into hotels, hiding under tables, and following the tour bus are frequent attempts, but the most daring was one smitten young lady who went for it suitcase-style, jumping on a baggage belt to get past airport security! As Britney Spears told the MTV Radio Network while she was touring with 'N Sync, "Oh my God, you should see these screaming girls. It's unreal. I mean, the things they do to see these guys is unbelievable."

'N Sync fans are nothing if not creative when it comes to showing their favorite band how devoted they are. Every day is Christmas for the 'N Sync five, as their fans bring gifts to every concert and send them presents in the mail. From Superman cakes and hand-knitted sweaters, poems, basketballs, and Beanie Babies to handcrafted miniatures of the band onstage and home videos of themselves lip-syncing to 'N Sync, the fans love to give something personal

back to thank the band for their great music. Of course the band can't keep all of the gifts they receive from their adoring fans–they would have a convoy of tour buses by now–so they donate all of the teddy bears, toys, and stuffed animals to children's hospitals.

The group has a lot of respect for their fans. "I think we really don't separate our fans into age groups, but I can tell you when it comes to littler kids we never talk down to them. . . . Kids are smart. We don't treat them like kids, we treat them like human beings," Chris revealed in his March 4, 1999, Yahoo chat session.

'N Sync fans do come in all ages, and some of them are as famous as the band members themselves. Kathy Griffin, the red-headed comedienne and co-star of Brooke Shields's hit TV series *Suddenly Susan*, has a running joke with the guys in 'N Sync, and tells everyone from MTV to Howard Stern that she is dating Joey. "Joey's 21, and he thinks I'm 28, and that's fine for everybody," she told *MTV News's* Chris Connelly. Joey's comeback, via MTV's John Norris, was to say that he and Kathy have been "married four years, have three kids, and live in Omaha, Nebraska." Fellow musical artist Ginuwine traveled to Florida just to meet 'N Sync and discuss recording a song or two together. "We kicked it off," he told MTV. "They're real cool guys, they're down to earth. Me and them were talking about duets and stuff like that and we spent about a week together. It was cool."

But back to the not-so-well-known ever-growing mass of loyal 'N Sync fans. A December 28, 1998, New York *Times* article entitled "The Roar of the Crowd" on the phenomena of screaming fans quoted an 'N Sync fan outside the MTV *Total Request Live* studios in New York City's Times Square. The fan, Karen La Plante, said, "I'm 18, so I'm not a teeny-bopper. I don't know what it is, but I just love 'N Sync. I've taken some pictures of Joey's arm, his head, Lansten's arm. All you see is yellow and red and blue, but it's worth it." Another, younger fan, fourteen-year-old Karen Lopez, was quoted as explaining, "Sometimes you say you're not going to scream, but then you do. . . . You're there, and then you start screaming, and then you scream some more. Your head hurts when you're finished, but you don't notice it while you're out here doing it." Well, J.C. may have put it best on the *'N Sync* enhanced CD when he said with a grin, "It's not exactly Beatlemania, but it's pretty cool."

THE LOOK

So what is it about these five guys that drives their fans so crazy? We know their music is truly special, and their live shows are out of this world, but there is something about 'N Sync that you can't put your finger on . . . they try very hard to be accessible and grounded and, well, normal, but the fact remains that they have that superstar quality that is hard to come by.

The band's style is what J.C. dubs "conservative chaos." From Canadian designer Parasuco, Guess, and Fubu to Nike to Fila to DKNY to Adidas . . . Justin described the 'N Sync look to *SuperTeen* magazine as "pretty diverse. I think we can go from being very athletic to very dressed up. Some of us are a little more hip-hop and some of us are a little more dressy." When the band makes a bit of an effort to get formal and discards the sporty gear, their individual fashion senses come to light. J.C. favors tasteful leather jackets and, in keeping with his more conservative, classic hairstyle, rarely wears anything outrageous or too flashy (aside from the time the guys all dressed up as seventies groovers, complete with afro wigs, that is!). Lance is also a subtle dresser, leaning toward earth tones and forest greens, but there's one thing he always wears—his angelic smile. Justin goes for his all-time fave color, baby blue, even when he's wearing a suit, and pairs his outfits with color-coordinated sunglasses. Getting down to the wilder end of the spectrum, we find Joey, Jr., in bright reds, attention-grabbing accessories, and the infamous leopard-print overcoat he carried off with that mischievous grin of his. And the award for the all-out, over-the-top voguester of them all goes to Chris, hands down. His wild and unique hairstyle is just the icing on the cake for a guy who manages to pull together furry hats, gold lame, psychedelic swirls, patterned head-kerchiefs, and a touch of velvet to fab effect.

Of course, 'N Sync have developed their group image over the years. The original video for "I Want You Back" provides an interesting look at the band at the very beginning. The video, shot in a studio, features a younger-looking group of five guys—including a braidless Chris—who aren't as comfortable with themselves as the ultra-confident, free-spirited 'N Sync of today. Their dancing is less sophisticated and seems to lack the originality and spark of the group we all know and love. It seems the band realized this themselves, and when they set their sights on the U.S.A., they decided to reshoot the video to better represent what they had become. The U.S. video showcases the band's personality, showing the guys playing pool, basketball, and jet skiing. It has a bit of a story-line, as shots of J.C. driving the other four band members around, just cruising, are intermixed with shots of him dropping an angry girlfriend off at home.

The video for "Here We Go" has as its theme a game close to the

band's hearts: basketball. The on-court dance routine set in a high school gym is a lot of fun, and features a few of 'N Sync's signature pranks, including Lance hiding the ball under his shirt and Joey getting hit right on the head with it! "Here We Go" was slated to be the theme song for the NBA in 1998, but unfortunately due to the lockout it didn't come to be. Ah well, at least 'N Sync had their own basketball team, complete with red, white, and blue 'N Sync uniforms, at MTV's *Rock 'N Jock* in Malibu, California. Justin sported a gold 'N Sync necklace to complement his jersey. His team number? 1 1/2!

The "Tearin' Up My Heart" video made a permanent mark on the MTV airwaves, and really established the band as personalities. As Chris says in the *'N the Mix* official home video, "We don't consider ourselves anything but five guys doing what we love to do and having the time of our lives doing it, so with that we try to portray that as much as possible in the video." And that they did, with the photo-shoot premise of the video showing the guys at wardrobe and make-up, eating pizza, and just having fun. Of course, the slick performance side of things gets its time as well, and the segment featuring Justin singing on an iron bed clinched his heartthrob label for once and for all.

It was Chris's idea to set the "(God Must Have Spent) A Little More Time on You" video in the forties. The black and white video is really a mini-movie, and shows the love between a mother and son grow over the years, as the son grows up, falls in love, and goes to war. The surprise ending of the video is a great touch. 'N Sync shot the video at Blair High School in Pasadena, California, and during the shoot Joey realized that one of the female extras was actually a girl he knew from high school!

In the video for "The Girl Who Has Everything" the band enacts the song's story. The fivesome find themselves shipwrecked on a beautiful tropical island, and while they cavort in the waves, horseback ride on the beach, and play in waterfalls, the "Girl Who Has Everything" is miserably celebrating her birthday in her fabulous New York City home, being showered with expensive gifts that mean nothing to her. Finally, she wanders down to the river only to find the bottle the boys threw into the ocean, containing a photo of the guys inscribed with *"For the girl who has everything / I bring you love."*

Maybe it is the very fact that this hot group is made up of five very unique individuals that makes 'N Sync so intriguing and irresistible to their fans. Their very different personalities blend together so well to form such a strong bond, but it is their distinctive characters that spark so much interest above and beyond their music. To help fans answer the ultimate question, "Who's your favorite?" . . .

JUSTIN

Justin Randall Timberlake, born January 31, 1981, the baby of the group, is most often referred to as the band's number one heartthrob. Born in Memphis, Tennessee, he exhibited musical talent before he could even walk, keeping time to whatever music his parents would play. His father, Randy, was in a bluegrass band, and little Justin began harmonizing along almost before he could talk. Singing in church was a great joy to him. His first taste of pop star style performance came along when he was in the fourth grade and formed a New Kids on the Block lip-syncing act with some friends. At age eleven he performed a country song on *Star Search*, and it wasn't long before he landed a two-year-long spot on The *Mickey Mouse Club*. Of course, he had his mischievous side as a kid. As he admitted to *SuperTeen* in the magazine's June 1999 issue, "I was like Ferris Bueller. So if someone got in trouble, they always made sure they got in trouble with me, because I was in good with the teachers. I was a big negotiator."

The tallest member of the group, Justin, with his blue eyes and curly blonde hair, has natural good looks. However, he doesn't take his looks too seriously. He has dyed his hair almost every color of the rainbow, including red, blonde, green, and, of course, his favorite shade, baby blue. He's addicted to diamond earrings, sneakers, basketball (one of his idols is Michael Jordan), and cereal. Everyone knows not to speak to Justin until he's had his cereal–it's the only thing that wakes him up. Until he's downed a bowl of Oreos drowned in milk he's just sleepwalking! The kid in him is still alive and kicking: his favorite cartoon character is Bugs

Bunny. Justin's fears are the three S's . . . spiders, snakes, and sharks, and his pet peeve is dishonesty. His hobbies include meditating, using his new lap-top, and writing songs and poetry.

Justin is a self-professed family man, and values the time he can spend with

his mom and stepdad and his father and stepmother. He absolutely adores his two stepbrothers. He spoke about his five-year-old brother, Jonathan, in *SuperTeen* magazine's June 1999 issue, saying, "It's so fun to watch him. I'll be sitting with my daddy and he's like, that's exactly how you were at that age. Jonathan can sing so well. He's got perfect pitch and he already hears harmonies and stuff." Jonathan reportedly goes to every 'N Sync concert he can! Steven, Justin's youngest brother, is only a baby and too young to realize that his big bro is a famous musical artist.

Okay, so let's get down to what every female 'N Sync fan who counts Justin as their fave really wants to know. What kind of person is he looking for in a girlfriend? "Confident, with a sense of humor, good listener, somebody with a sensitive heart," is how Justin described his perfect mate during his February 12, 1999, Yahoo chat. "I am a hopeless romantic, and I don't get off on people who make fun of other people. Somebody I could learn from, that would complement me, that could help me grow as a person." Justin's ideal girl is optimistic about life. He feels that there is too much pessimism in the world today. What about his first kiss? Justin admitted, "I was nervous. And I was with my girlfriend at that time. It was funny, now that I look back on how nervous I was. I wouldn't call it love, I would call it an infatuation. I think when you're in love with somebody you know it for sure." As unbelievable as it sounds to his fans, this heartthrob's only experience with real love (yet) was actually heartbreaking. He met her in 1995 at a party through mutual *MMC* buds. "Everything between us fitted in a minute! I was in love over both ears," Justin admitted to *Faces in Pop* magazine in its Winter Special '99 issue. "She ended it, she was secretly meeting with another boy. To me, it felt like my world collapsed–I was so hurt and sad! I had love pain for several months." Justin confesses to being a little gun-shy about falling head over heels again, although at this point in his life he's much too busy to fit a love affair into his schedule!

JOEY

Joseph Anthony Fatone, Jr., was born (January 28, 1977) and raised in Brooklyn, New York, in a loving family. His father was a major influence on Joey Junior's desire to sing and perform; Joey's father sang in the Orions, a doo-wop group who performed all over New York and New Jersey. He was also very involved in the church and local theater, and would organize an annual Christmas show, which involved acting and music; needless to say, his son was happy to participate. Joey has been a ham ever since he was a toddler! Joey's early days were

filled with the sounds of the Temptations and Frankie Lymon and the Teenagers, as well as more contemporary groups like Boyz II Men. The stylish Joey of today attended a Catholic school called St. Mary's as a kid, and had to wear a uniform and tie every day.

When Joey had just turned a teenager, he, his parents, and his sister Janine and brother Steven moved to Orlando, Florida. When Joey first went to Florida, his father tricked him into it! Joe Fatone, Sr., told his kids that he was going on a business trip, and suggested that they come with him to the airport to see the inside of an airplane for the first time. It wasn't until the captain announced that it was time to fasten seatbelts in preparation for take-off that Joey's parents told their children that in fact they were all off to sunny Florida! The kids had fallen lock, stock, and barrel for the prank—they didn't even realize that their parents had packed suitcases for them!

It was in Orlando that Joey began to seriously develop his acting, dancing, and singing talent. He acted in *Matinee* and *SeaQuest*, but his favorite acting stint to date was his small part in the film *Once upon a Time in America*. He told *Celebrity Series Presents* magazine, "I was honored to play that role simply because the story was fantastic and I got to act in the same film as my idol Robert DeNiro." As luck would have it, he landed a gig at Universal Studios after high school—and we all know where that led.

Nowadays Joey's full-time job is performing, but his hobbies have remained the same. As any 'N Sync fan knows, Joey is crazy about Superman and collects any memorabilia he can get his hands on. He may wear Superman shirts and a Superman necklace today, but as a kid he wore a cape—and even tried to fly, which earned him more than a few scrapes and bruises. He loves going clubbing, going to the movies, and just hanging out with his friends. His favorite food? Italian, of course. Joey also gets a thrill out of traveling, and when on the road with 'N Sync he discovered that he loved South Africa and Asia, and was very impressed with Germany's architecture.

What about girls? Joey is known as the flirt of the group, but he made a surprising confession during his December 10, 1998, Yahoo chat. He claimed, "I got dumped on my first date! I took her to the movies. And she dumped me!" He added with his typical good humor, "I guess the movie wasn't that good." Joey has a great sense of humor—you can tell by his smile—and doesn't take anything too seriously. He doesn't mind making fun of himself. When *Tiger Beat* magazine asked Joey about his favorite body part, he said, "The worst is my feet—because I step on everything. Best? My nose, because it's big and I can smell a lot of food." When asked on Yahoo what one thing he couldn't do without, Joey jokingly replied, "Clothes. I wouldn't want to run around naked." Most importantly, Joey knows it is important to remain grounded despite 'N Sync's overwhelming success. Joey confessed in his March 11, 1999, Yahoo chat that he can't let fame go to his head, saying, "All of us keep each other on the ground and if I had a chip on my shoulder or a big head about this . . . my mom would kick my butt!"

J.C.

It is difficult for fans of the confident, heartfelt singer J.C. (Joshua Scott Chasez, born in Washington, D.C., on August 8, 1976) to believe that he grew up a very shy guy. It was only his love of the dancing styles of M.C. Hammer and Bell Biv Devoe that really got him into all of this. He was dared by some female friends to enter a dance competition with them, and lo and behold, they won! He soon recovered from his bashfulness, and got up the courage to sing—and could he ever sing. His very first audition for anything was for the *Mickey Mouse Club*, and he was one of ten kids chosen from 20,000 who gave it a shot, and was on the show for four fulfilling years.

It seems that J.C. was just biding his time as a kid, enjoying a normal family life with his parents, sister Heather, and brother Tyler. Some of his favorite memories are very adventurous family vacations. He told *SuperTeen* magazine, "We always went and did wild and weird road trips. We were like the Griswalds from *National Lampoon's Family Vacation* . . . we would drive anywhere . . . we've seen freak shows on Route 66, we've seen it all." J.C. wanted to be a carpenter or an architect or an antique car restorer when he was younger, but 'N Sync fans are thankful that none of those career choices worked out.

His hobbies today include collecting Hard Rock Café menus, and he wears a lion necklace in honor of his star sign, Leo. He loves all of the Star Wars movies; in fact, his first crush was Star Wars' Princess Leia! Restless J.C. brings a yo-yo on tour with him. As Justin told *Faces in Pop* magazine, "J.C.'s always moving—he has to be dancing around or doing something in the background." Despite all of his energy, the band call him Sleepy Spice; he's the first to admit that 'N Sync's grueling schedule doesn't give him much time for one of his favorite pastimes—a little shut-eye.

J.C.'s sculpted cheekbones and soulful eyes are enough to make any girl sigh. However, the good-looking J.C. is attracted to someone who is secure with themselves, and not hung up on how they look. He described his ideal date on Yahoo, saying it would have to be "somewhere quiet. So I can get to know that person. I don't need a lot of noise and hype and all that. I want to be able to chat and get to know each other."

First and foremost, J.C. is a perfectionist, and a true professional. He sticks to his principles no matter what. "I wouldn't go on TV grabbing this, that, or the other and have my parents looking at that," J.C. told *People Online* in its February 8, 1999, issue. "That's just the way I was raised." He's also been called Serious Spice, and the fact that he takes his role as a pop star and entertainer very seriously indeed is one key to his success.

CHRIS

Christopher Alan Kirkpatrick, the oldest member of 'N Sync—and the one who came up with the fantastic idea of the band in the first place—was born in Clarion, Pennsylvania, on October 17, 1971. He comes from a very, very musical family. Both sets of his great-grandparents were in bands; his grandmother was an opera singer; his grandfather was a country and western singer who recorded five albums; his aunts and uncles are in bands from country, rock, and jazz to rockabilly; and his mother teaches voice lessons and plays several instruments. How's that for having music in the blood?

Chris was always getting himself into something as a kid—it looks like things haven't changed. He has a scar over his left eye, which he got while misbehaving as a youngster; he was chasing his sister and hit a wall. "I was a serious kid," Chris jokingly told *SuperTeen* magazine in its May 1999 issue. "No, I was a trouble-maker! I was rambunctious. I was real hyper. But I was always into music. I loved music. I've got pictures, I've got little films of me singing, doing Oliver Twist, doing all these little musi-cals." In high school Chris had lead roles in many school plays. He graduated from Orlando's Valencia Community College in 1993, the same school Backstreet Boy Howie Dorough attended. Although Chris loves the music industry, and always had it in his mind to pursue a career as a performer, he seriously considered becoming a psychologist, and majored in psychology in addition to his theater and music classes.

Chris is definitely the craziest member of 'N Sync. In keeping with his reputation, he even goofed on the typist helping him out during his Yahoo chat by stating that his New Year's Resolution was "To stop saying supercalifragilisticexpialidocious." When another fan asked him if he believed in aliens, claiming to be the victim of an abduction, Chris replied, "Hmmm . . . So was I . . . Let's go seek counseling together" and was quick to come up with being "force fed cooked carrots" as his least favorite activity. He then jokingly described his method for escaping fan attention, saying, "I can't really disguise myself. I dress up as Justin some-times–that seems to work." When asked who would play him in a movie, Chris comes up with Bette Midler. He loves tacos, and has named himself Refried Bean Spice.

The story of Chris's first kiss came out online, during his Yahoo chat. Even when it comes to love, Chris can't help but joke around. He claimed, "It was awk-ward b/c we were playing Kiss Tag so after she kissed me she punched me. So had to learn at a very young age that women are nothing but trouble ;-)."

The guy with the wild hairstyle and endless energy loves children and takes his role as a performer very seriously indeed. His psychology studies helped him learn about music therapy and how good music is for the soul; he knows the power of music. He loves to chill out in his spare time (if he ever has any) and spin records on his turntable. He carries a small Indian shield and a cross with him for good luck. Chris told 'N Sync fans on Yahoo, "I'd love to be a tree, because trees just seem so knowledgeable and such a permanent thing on earth."

Chris may be known as a jokester, always handy with a quick comeback or a witty answer, but he remains, underneath it all, very serious about what matters. When asked by *Celebrity Series Presents* about fame, he replied, "Being famous means changing and we don't want that to happen. It is our job to stay grounded and not to change our personalities." He went on to say, "Our aim is to be good, as good as we can be, but we also have to be individuals."

{forty-three}

LANCE

The mellow, calm, and relaxed Lance wasn't always that way. It seems that James Lance Bass, born on May 4, 1979, in Clinton, Mississippi, was quite a handful! He confessed to *SuperTeen* magazine that he "was like a really crazy idiot when I was little. I was very hyper; that's all I loved to do was just play and play. I was just a little comedian —everyone was like, 'You're gonna grow up to be a comedian.' And then I really matured and now I'm laid back. I totally changed." It must be in honor of his earlier manic days that Lance's pet mascot today is the Tasmanian Devil.

It has been reported that Lance came close to his original career dream of becoming an astronaut by passing the NASA entrance examination! We do know that he attended Space Camp at Camp Kennedy when he was in the seventh grade. He told *SuperTeen* magazine that the experience "was so much fun. After that, I was just like, that's what I want to do. We had to simulate shuttle missions and all that kind of stuff. It was incredible. I loved the whole thing." Lance used to work at a daycare center in Mississippi until he received that fateful phone call from Justin's vocal coach. He played baseball, football, and basketball at school, and his favorite subjects were science and math. He still keeps at his academics, taking courses through the University of Nebraska. Lance collects Beanie Babies, plays keyboards, and reads the Bible in his spare time. He is a water person, and loves jet skiing and water-skiing.

Green-eyed Lance is looking for a girl with whom he could be close friends first, with the hope that the relationship would blossom over time into something more. He revealed during his Yahoo chat what his ideal female companion would be, saying, "I like the innocent type. The good girls. I like a religious girl. Someone I can talk to and be best friends with for anything."

He truly seems to relish the opportunity to see the world; as he says in the *'N the Mix* official home video, "Being on tour is one of the highlights of being in this business—getting to travel all over the world, getting to see city after city, meet new people . . . it's an incredible feeling." Lance loved Liechtenstein "because it's the most peaceful country you'll probably ever go to," he reminisced during his Yahoo chat session, calling it "just paradise." Most people go to tropical islands in order to relax, but not Lance. During his trip to Cancun he ended up in a bullfight! And he will be the first to tell you that it was an extremely painful and frightening experience. Maybe next time he'll just soak up the sun and read a good book.

Lance's nickname, Scoop, was given to him by Joey's brother Steve, who relies on Lance to keep him up-to-date on the band's activities as Lance always memorizes the 'N Sync itinerary. And it's no secret

that Lance has a head for business, and is extremely interested in all of the behind-the-scenes music industry operations behind the creation and maintenance of a successful band like 'N Sync. Joey described Lance in *Teen Dream* magazine's April 1999, issue, saying, "He's such a good person to talk to. He's really knowledgeable about business and marketing and is always on top of things." Here's just one example: Lance, the future industry executive, showed his head for business when it came to the band's next single. RCA had "For the Girl Who Has Everything" slated as the next hit, but Lance mentioned that he felt that most fans' favorite was "(God Must Have Spent) A Little More Time on You" and that he thought it would be wise to switch choices. The record company took Lance's suggestion seriously enough to launch an online contest in which fans could vote on the band's next single—and guess which song came out way on top! Maybe next time they'll pay heed to Lance's hunches!

After their four-year long whirlwind rise to incredible success, you would think 'N Sync is due for a nice, long vacation. A bit of time on the beach, a chance to shoot some hoops, see a few movies, hang out with friends and family. Right? Wrong! Don't forget, this is a group that thrives on hard work, and a group that absolutely adores every aspect of their musical career—performing, recording, meeting fans . . . they plan to make the very most of it.

So, even before the 'N Sync five set out on their three-month headlining Spring tour, the exciting announcement was made that the band was planning a very special treat to help their fans have a great summer. Yes, the band that never stops has the most ambitious tour yet up their sleeves. They've decided to go all out, and all male! The Boys of Summer Tour has 'N Sync pairing up with Irish boy band Five and Jordan Knight, former New Kids on the Block member gone solo. The tour is to be launched in Virginia Beach the day after Fourth of July fireworks, and is scheduled to run all of the way through the end of August . . . it promises to be one hot show.

And just in case that's not enough to keep the ever-expanding rank of 'N Sync-crazy fans happy, the band will release a brand new album just in time to stop the back-to-school blues. The album is due out in September/October, and the first single is slated to hit the airwaves in July, during the tour. The band recorded the album in Burbank, California, with producer Guy Roche (of Celine Dion fame). The band is also working with Diane Warren, the Grammy-winning songwriter behind Lee Ann Rhimes' hit "How Do I Live." It's rumored that the new album also includes a ballad called "That's When I'll Stop Loving You."

'N Sync love the idea of collaborating with other artists, and have named the likes of Busta Rhymes, Leann Rimes, Jewel, Janet Jackson, and Gwen Stefani (although Chris claims he could never sing a duet with her as he'd be too busy asking her out on a date!) as part of their wish list for partners in music. They recently recorded a song with an artist they all admire, Phil Collins. The 'N Sync guys got a taste of how their fans must feel when they met Mr. Collins and laid down a track together for the *Tarzan* soundtrack.

Yes, 'N Sync have certainly come a long way from their humble beginnings as five young guys with a dream and a lot of determination. The days when Joey's mother, Phyllis, stored the band's fan mail in her living room are long gone. Justin's mother now owns her own management company in Orlando. Chris is branching out with his own clothing line called Fu Man Skeeto—he will sell his young, hip-hop clothes online on a web site. Lance has already begun fulfilling his bandmates' prophesy about his business acumen future. He has

just launched his own management company, cleverly christened Free Lance Entertainment, and his first artist is a country singer named Meredith Edwards. To celebrate, he is looking for a house in Orlando on the water. Television pilots are allegedly being written for the boys, and movie plans are a major subject of discussion. Oh, and they have just been given their own day. Yes, you heard right: New Haven, Connecticut named Saturday, March 13, "'N Sync Day" and made it official at a ceremony headed by the State Representative, who presented the band with a proclamation.

All signs say that 'N Sync is here to stay. They realize that the music industry is a fickle business, but they feel confident that their talent and strengths will evolve even further as their career develops. They plan to build on a very solid base. "As far as being type cast, that's just something we have to break the mold over time," J.C. explained during his January 13, 1999, Yahoo chat. "The only way we can is to stick around awhile until we're not boys anymore! And as far as competition, we compete with ourselves." Chris told *People Online* in its February 8, 1999, issue, "We're not going to pierce everything that we have and paint our faces trying to get a different market. We'll grow with our audience. We're just going to keep doing what we do." For 'N Sync fans, that's the best news yet!

DISCOGRAPHY:

ALBUMS:
'N SYNC
3/24/98 USA; RCA 676131
Tearin' Up My Heart / I Just Wanna Be with You / Here We Go / For the Girl Who Has Everything / (God Must Have Spent) A Little More Time On You / You Got It / I Need Love / I Want You Back / Everything I Own / I Drive Myself Crazy / Crazy for You / Sailing / Giddy Up

HOME FOR CHRISTMAS
11/10/98 USA; RCA 67726
Home for Christmas / Under My Tree / I Never Knew the Meaning of Christmas / Merry Christmas, Happy Holidays/ The Christmas Song (Chestnuts Roasting on an Open Fire)/ I Guess It's Christmas Time/ All I Want Is You This Christmas/ The First Noel / In Love on Christmas / It's Christmas / O Holy Night (A Cappella) / Love's in Our Hearts on Christmas Day / The Only Gift / Kiss Me at Midnight

WINTER ALBUM
11/98 European; BMG International 58816
U Drive Me Crazy / (God Must Have Spent) A Little More Time On You / Thinking Of You / Everything I Own / I Just Wanna Be With You / Family Affair / Kiss Me At Midnight / Merry Christmas, Happy Holidays / All I Want Is You (This Christmas) / Under My Tree / Love's In Our Hearts On Christmas / In Love On Christmas / The First Noel

'N SYNC
Germany; BMG International 471641.
Tearin' up My Heart / You Got It / Sailing / Crazy for You / Riddle / For the Girl Who Has Everything / I Need Love / Giddy Up / Here We Go / Best of My Life / More Than a Feeling /I Want You Back / Together Again / Forever Young

SINGLES:
I WANT YOU BACK
11/98 Germany; BMG International 41679

U DRIVE ME CRAZY
1998 Europe; BMG International 58815

I WANT YOU BACK
12/98 Australia; BMG International 65330

I WANT YOU BACK/ GIDDY UP
2/98 USA; RCA 65348

I WANT YOU BACK (5 tracks)
2/98 USA; RCA 65373

COMPILATIONS/APPEARANCES:
SABRINA, THE TEENAGE WITCH SOUNDTRACK
(Various Artists)
Geffen 25220, October 1998
Walk Of Life - Spice Girls / Abracadabra - Sugar Ray / Hey, Mr. DJ (Keep Playin' This Song) - Backstreet Boys / One Way Or Another - Melissa Joan Hart / Kate - Ben Folds Five / Show Me Love (Radio Edit) - Robyn / Giddy Up - 'N Sync / Slam Dunk (Da Funk) - Five / Magnet & Steel - Matthew Sweet / So I Fall Again - Phantom Planet / I Know What Boys Like - Pure Sugar / Smash - The Murmurs, Jane Wiedlin, Charlotte Caffey / Dr. Jones (Metro 7In Edit) - Aqua / Soda Pop - Britney Spears / Amnesia (Radio Remix) - Chumbawamba / Blah, Blah, Blah - The Cardigans